The Raven's Poison

Collected Poems

Braeden Michaels

The Raven's Poison

Collected Poems

Braeden Michaels

Storm of Ink
2020

This book is a work of poetry.

First paperback edition April 2020

Front cover design by bookcoverzone.com

ISBN 978-1-7347499-0-8 (paperback)

Published by Storm of Ink
PO Box 152
Gainesville, GA USA 30503
www.braedenmichaels.com

PREFACE

Before you begin to read *"The Raven's Poison"* it is imperative to understand the essence of this collection. As a child I begin to write lines of poetry on a post-it notes. My mother would come across them and often would hang them on the refrigerator. She was the only one who truly encouraged me to write. She was able to recognize something I couldn't see for a long time. I spent years playing hide and seek with this silent passion. It wasn't until my mid-thirties where it became evident that I could no longer hide it.

Once I discovered that writing was a huge part of me it became apparent to me, I didn't want to be "just" a published author. I wanted my poetry to feel and appear to be different. I began to challenge myself as a writer with the style. A friend of mine coined a term (*Deconstructive Literature*) with a certain style of my writing of poems. It's considered to be a new form of poetry.

Deconstructive Literature: The author takes a thought, idea, scene, emotion and deconstructs it only to rebuild it again, piece by piece, line upon line. Pulling out hidden flavors here and accentuating unknown colors there. Drawing one's attention to the underlying scent and undiscovered textures. The author mixes and remixes, not relying on conventional phrases or images, but rather pulls from something one might see from the corner of their eye instead. Glimpses and flashes that make up the whole. Each line or thought building upon the previous one, brick stacked on brick, to achieve that final goal bringing the reader in to not only visualize but also taste, smell, and hear the author's intended idea.

This compilation of poetry touches every emotion that all of us feel. Although most of this collection is dark, the content's purpose is to create reflection in the reader's mind. As humans we often stare into the past and we are unable to grasp a state of mind. It takes a past to change the present or future. This collection stares into most of the pitch-black emotions: anger, lust, shattered hearts, and self-destruction. On the other side of the dark there is the light. It touches every shade of love: self-love, spirituality, and being in love without any judgement. It takes the light to appreciate the essence of the dark.

DEDICATION

Thank you, mother, for believing in me. I can feel and hear you when I am writing. I am who I am because of you.

Thank you all for the support.

TABLE OF CONTENTS

SOUL'S COLORS

"The colors of the soul are made up of the rainbow."

The Ballerina in the Snow Globe

She dances like a ballerina in a snow globe
Dandelions are adding
lyrics to the sound of Mozart
The splashes of watercolors were hanging above her elegance
She glides for forgiveness
and sways for sobriety
The tinsel around her fury spirit is no longer sparkling
She is twirling and spinning for a numb audience
The atmosphere is toxic
The ambiance in the snow globe is desolate
At the end of the ballet only one rose was thrown
in front of her feet
God threw it with all his might
Her tears fell to the floor like a tidal wave
She only needed to dance for herself

Scraping Arrogance

Slapping the vanity
Presumptuous to the brim
Scalding hot from the smugness
Overbearing and trite
Turning the nail to the left
like a screw in a headboard
Watching the confidence
disappear into consequences
Fabrications built like kingdoms
Casting out disdain and remarks
Scraping the bottom layer
Pounding the nerves of arrogance
Seeking hollow praise
Self-worshipping a glass chin
Bound to shatter soon

Faded Signature

Congested on fabrication
Summarizing chaos
Condensing ignorance
Abbreviating points of view
Pondering quick judgement
Oblivious first impressions
Downsizing the circle
Maximum serenity
Reducing nonsense
Following instincts
Sketching visions
Recognizing the difference
between acquaintances
and loyalists

Nighthawk Masquerade

The ballroom is filled with chaos debutantes and stainless-steel soldiers
The greetings were choreographed by a comedian
The chandelier hangs over the melting pot with Cadillac dreams
The laughter is just as fake as a plastic credit card
Sipping on lies and guzzling down the shadows of reality
The honor among thieves is the ace of spades
Plagiarism shines in the corners
as the compliments are memorized from a hallmark card
The truth never strutted through the double doors
The costumes reek of mediocrity and the dialogue is stale
The pride never appears as the tap shoes dance all through the hours
Berlin and Chopin soar in the air as the feet move in sync
As the night ends all of them become strangers
They entered wearing a mask and
leave being someone they always wanted to be

The Lost Scarecrow

Through the autumn fields
the dark sky casts shadows of summer
A lightning bolt
strikes at midnight
The bewitched scarecrow
crawls out of the isolated barn
The monster inside
the scarecrow is now awakened
The child inside
the beast screams for his mother
His mother of reason's
skin has become ashes
The agony that the scarecrow
holds becomes weight
on his shoulders
Time has made him
the lost scarecrow
no peace was made with his loss
The lost scarecrow's heart
has melted away
He lives in the barn where
he has watched his mother
cry oceans of pain
The lost scarecrow has finally
made it to the lake of change
He closes his eyes of anguish
and falls into the lake
to wash away the burden
He is now sitting on
the dock with flesh reborn

Symphony and the Sea

She played the sound of jazz
until the late hours
She played the fond memories in her head
like a CD and
kept hitting the button repeat
She played the heartache and
forgot her destination
She played the sound of silence
as the words were jumbled in her head
She played the acoustic guitar
to the rhythm of her soothing soul
She played the chorus
to the ballerina dancing to
the edge of her heart
She played for many
but lost the sight of her identity
She finally played for herself and
could feel the symphony
She could calm the sea within her beauty

Twisted Whispers

Black clouds
flow over the callous winds
A thousand leaves
twist in the cold
Solitude turns
into autumn chaos
The thirst
for the calm is
naked and fearless
Tremors and the twitching
of recklessness are carved
Whispers of your words
leave me speechless
The illusions become
more corrupt
Fabricated
as he swallows
more liquid disease

Whispers Goodbye

I was sucker punched
with the lack of sensitivity
I stood in a marble corner
in thick shackles
aching for over the top affection
I took a left hook to the jaw
from a decaying prisoner of stone-cold truth
As my body fell to the
shallow and devious ocean
I saw myself drown because I'm an inconvenience
Bruises from loneliness, cracked ribs
from your ballistic and absurd point of view
Barely breathing from you cramming down
your ideologies
Whispering goodbye

Darkest Fairy Tale

Once upon a lightless sky
the breeze was suffocating just like the words
that sit in the back of my throat
It was almost as if a magician waved
his wand upon my head
The darkest fairytale only has a splash of glitter
but filled with sorrow
Lately I am being
reflective but in a trance
The revelation is near
The path of resistance is in my clenched fist
The branches hang just like my arms
The words that stutter drift into the sleepless nights
Into the white discussions your words appear
The meanings and the symbolism are quite transparent
We are shuffling our feet in this darkest fairytale
The magician has gone home
and all that is left in this room is our truth

Twilight and Fire

Blazing flames
of hope are ignited
Believe in
your essence

Stars of dreams
fill the heavenly
skies above the vast ocean
Believe in
the light of the future

Dripping gold
is tangled around
the center of your being
Believe in
your magnetic passion

Your eyes
are not wide
enough to see
Believe in
the power of your destiny

Turning points
sparkle like twilight and wildfire
Believe in
your faded scars

From Above and Outward

Breathtaking hallucinations
Flying without aluminum wings
Treasuring the peaks and valleys
Admiring the crystal meadow

Distinctly harboring the flashes
Mesmerizing the spheres
In awe of the radiance and glow
Caught up in the photographic glance

Staring at the vanishing mirror
Finally opening my eyes to the light
Seeing new beginnings
Drawing lines of all the endings

Chapters divided and separated by victories
Losses are no longer crippling
Deciding to see the glass half full than empty
Entering a clear atmosphere

Spray Paint

Erratic and frantic
Colors of love blend
Assumptions
Killing your spirit
Relinquish
your demands
Walking upon a
vanishing tightrope
above your sanity
Not cognitive
of the words you spoke
A new picture
has been created
to force you to think
about your being
Constantly hiding
behind the spray
painted heart

Inside the Blood Clot

I scratched my identity
with a worn 1974 penny
I saw moisture dripping
from my divided reflection
Murky colors and shades
of discomfort twitch
Uncontrollable jitters
Apathy is a phobia suspended
over my troubled head
A hemorrhage spread out
from the corners to the end
Lack of intersections and interest
Bent and upended against
paralyzed and indifferent nerves
I saw the gash and blemishes
inside the blood clot
I abandoned the rustic door
and sit inside the character
No one wishes to see exist

Spilled Ink

Crimson outlines
Horrendous headlines
A catatonic massacre
Dried up sensationalism
Lipstick metaphors
Drizzling suicide letters
Heartbreaking mourning
Blinding by torn secrets
Never ending blood stains
Unexplainable motivations
In a barbed wire prison

Tangerine Slippers

Constantly chuckling
Flirting with the chauffeur
Wiping away the cookie crumbs
with her red satin glove
Refined but down to the ground
Comprehending humans
the uplifting sister of Dr. Jekyll
Marching along the side
with the devious Mr. Hyde
Strolling in tangerine slippers
seeking simplicity in complexity
Parading the crowded streets
with greetings and handshakes
Removing the word "status"
from Abigail's stunning vocabulary
Wearing comfortable clothes
Not caring what others think
of her tangerine slippers

Whispering Feathers

Sparks fly
Unseen flames
A brilliant eye
Capturing still beauty
Western belle
Blazing passion
Mint wings of a
Magnificent bird
Born with a gift
Believe in your
Whispering feathers

Unleashed Chaos

Disturbing Black
Dry ink staring
Startled and confined
Unorthodox wisdom
No room for error
Touching the demise
Carefully trickling
Vanishing tranquility
Distorted stars
No sense of time
Deep irritations
Under the fingernail
Biting on truth
Waiting vigorously
No heartbeat existed
Unleashed chaos

Scared to Death

I'm scared to death of your love
I'm scared to death of your pull
I'm scared to death to reach inside
I'm scared to death of what you see
I'm scared to death of what you feel
I'm scared to death of the unknown
I'm scared to death of the uncertainty
I'm scared to death of your beauty
I'm scared to death of the height
I'm scared to death of the fall

Dancing Tsunami

The dramatist paints his words
like a trapeze artist that flies in the air
Words pouring out like a tsunami
in his wide opened mind
The poet captures the authenticity of the moment
He stands on the stage and lashes out to the crowd
The words cut dive and linger
in the air of the audience
He wishes to be profound thought provoking and abstract
The words dangle swim swerve and screech in spirit
The dancing poet embarks on a path to the circus of lights
The light shines on the tears of the poet
The fragile heart of the poet is captivated by the silence
Someone wants to see beyond his words
Someone wants to see what underneath is

Forgotten Daughter

I'm a rag doll
with deteriorating veins
Melancholy is my
vodka guzzling down
my parched throat
Second prize
is sewn to my
invisible forehead
I'm a lost princess
craving love and affection
Bleakness is the name
of my withering perfume
I stumble between sister Abigail
and Thanksgiving leftovers
the color of my eyes
has only seen mourning grey
and the slamming of doors
I write in my black
and white diary
In cursive you will see it
labeled as the forgotten daughter

Voiceless Ghost

Everlasting champagne skies
Dying cold waterfalls
Vivid colors of translucent dreams
Walking miracles laugh

Deep radiant horizons glare
Sunrises aching for shade
Fences surrounding fears
Trees covering the empty shadows

Lost joys of sipping wine
Sweethearts divide by words
Lovebirds fly away from each other
Flashbacks of butterflies singing

Memories of hands tangled
Serenading voice of trust
Quietly disappear like a ghost
Endings evaporate into beginnings

If Time Shatters

Clocks burst
If time implodes
Digits disperse
If time disappears
Deadlines separate
If time yells
Roman numerals cry
If time drifts
Gates of anxiety rattle
If time dwells
Doors of fears close
If time explodes
Nothing matters

A Table for Two

Innocently sitting
A table for two
Sleeping with the chapters
Blocking out sirens
Change dropping to the street
Erasing her ex's and lovers
Breathing in marinated chicken
Waiting patiently for her
Garden salad swimming in
a pool of ranch dressing
Crowds of fake gestures
walk by in navy and silver suits
Gazing at her long legs
Continuing to turn crisp pages
Blinded by "a table for two"
Only sitting one
Loneliness is inconclusive
Perhaps it's a choice

Catfish Syndrome

Tangled in the coral reef
Feet dangling an inch
above the sand
Fingertips above the salty
and dreary ocean
Squirming with a twenty
pound chain around
my pale and distorted neck
Aching to shed dead skin
Refusing to be a bottom feeder
Removing the dwelling term
Catfish Syndrome

Cold Hard Itch

I've scratched the surface
Seeking something I'm not good at being
Staring at the mirror is harder than I thought
The cold hard itch isn't what I want to feel
I've crumpled the paper
I have disliked the words that I have chosen
Staring at a page feeling like a chameleon
The cold hard itch isn't what I want to know
I've ignored the taste
Fearing what will swallow me whole
I am staring at a chapter that I treasure
The cold hard itch isn't what I expected

The Knave's Carousel

The hand of the angry tattered man
was raised above his barbaric head
He was stuck in his fictitious crumbling vision
The lies spun around on the carousel
and were unable to face the truth
His nails scratched at the coffin of deception
The veins of the knave became thin
as clarity washed over the walls of frustration
The carousel still spun as the fire within
burned all his precious memories
The soul of the barbarian was deteriorating
as he believed in his severed remains
The carousel slowed down
as the innocent leapt off realizing their fate

Rendezvous Shadow

I'm sorry for the restless carnage
I'm sorry for the bridge of hurt
I'm sorry for the never-ending wounds
I'm sorry for the blazing bullets
I'm sorry for the vicious disguise
I'm sorry for the rendezvous shadow
I'm sorry for the bloodletting
I'm sorry for the eclipse in your eye
I'm sorry for the circling thunder
I'm sorry for my cursed identity
I'm sorry for my numb existence

Lackluster

Pulled and tugged
Intoxicating moans vibrate
Caught up in the kerosene
Waving goodbye
Leaving for Los Angeles
New start new sensations
An overload of freshness
Scenery will alter a broken identity
A blonde overturned to a redhead
Changing everything but
Her tattered and caged soul
No matter what you change
On the outside
Lackluster is her first name

A Nemesis' Tantrum

I stand before
my screeching nemesis
I walk among
the stenciled names
I make the claim
that I'm a deserted poet
But my heart is
full of words of melancholy
I shrug my shoulders
in a tearful silence
I laugh at the jester
in the corridor
of my creative mind
But my heart is
full of colors from the
distant rainbows
I sit upright and stare
down the thirsty enemy
My words speak for
millions of people
I sit Indian style
with infinite words in ink

Unabashed

She scrawled until she was dizzy
Paragraphs of former lovers
She raised a glass of champagne
to her wrecking divorce
Cut off the emptiness
She stood in front of the
awkward silence and crying sunrise
She ignored the pointing fingers
of the masses
A tint of courage glares
She waved goodbye to her chain
and thoughtless pigeon
A flag of independence was raised
She opened the door to freedom
She ran outside the margins
Bounds were not outlined
She thought the glass was half empty
She tore the corner of her mind
Unveiling a book without a name
She saw a glimpse of a brave
and unabashed sphere

Chewing on Glass

Chewing on glass
Blood gushing from the corners
In the silent hour
Flying away from my hiatus
As I swallow bits of misery
Generated by my indifference
Apathy ingrained
Indulging character trips
Changing the scenery
Refusing to digress
Steadily evolving
The glass will make me

Sipping Moscato

Lingering conversations
drizzle around sipping Moscato
Deep into political debates
Analyzing the yin and the yang
Interpreting Shakespeare
Rolling eyes over reality TV
As we sit enduring the thunder
speaking of skeptics and cynics
while Muddy Waters is playing
Laughing at the dirty jokes
Crying over the Roaring 20's
Watching technology take over
As I cherish the taste of my wine

Voodoo Doll

Trapped in humdrum
Sipping a bottle of mundane
She's a voodoo doll
In the shoes of a routine
Removing the shine to
make me dull
She's a relentless beast
Stuck in lukewarm
Forced to be conventional
She's a haunted child
Slowly sucking the imagination
out of me
Determined to make me ordinary
She's doused in vanilla
Bending me to be apathetic
Breaking the essence of me
She's turning me inside out
to become what she is

Gracefully Torn

Chapters reopened
Staring at a trance
Catching a glimpse
to see every jagged flaw
Scattered memories
become a missing piece
to the majestic puzzle
Pages photographed
Inhaling every word
Catching a bird's eye view
to see the oceans sky
Exhaling to recognize
I'm gracefully torn

Picking up the Pieces

Staring at the rubble
Absorbing the aftershock
Slowly picking up the pieces
You become a disappearing act
Walking on shards of glass
Feeling the cuts on my feet
Determined to pick up the pieces
Wiping the dust from my
Furious eyes
Realizing I no longer want you

Rusty Thorns

A weeping transformation
Gliding obscurity
Soaring melancholy drifts
Disregarding intentions
Clasping to what was
Binding to a new-found love
Seeing hollow affection
Cradling the bottle of hope
Admiring your perception
Desiring to comprehend
what you saw in me
I saw glitter in your
diamond shaped soul
Forever it will sparkle
on the crisp edges
of my fragmented heart
Ignoring the rusty thorns

Do I Care Enough

Should I care enough
to acknowledge your existence
Do I care enough
to reply to your nonsense
Should I care enough
to slap that grin off your devious face
Do I care enough
to raise my palm toward an empty man
Should I care enough
to not leave you penniless
Do I care enough
to take you to court
Should I care enough
to walk away from you
Do I care enough
about myself to decide
Should I care enough
about myself to leave you

Broken Record

How many times
must I repeat myself?
You claim to listen
But you just hear
You are lost in touch
Forgot the beginning
Along the way
Your true color appeared
in front of me
We've come this far
I have an option
that never entered
your simple mind
We aren't going to
to throw away the
broken record
I will toss the record
player all by myself
so, you can play it
somewhere else

Piece of Cloud

Perception
is a piece of cloud
suspended
over a mime
juggling wishes
and razor-sharp truths
Among the
Bottom feeders and
ladder climbers
patience is a stellar drink
that only a few
will drink from the
enchanting cup
Who are you?

PIECES OF LOVE

"We all hide the pieces that make up the whole."

Ceramic Villains

Stomach acid
gorges the frame of the picture
Ceramic villains
stand in the center of the image
Credit card smiles
seek the light of the troubled road
Wallets become empty
as they cling to the objects of the rooms

Love was just a word to deceive

Camouflaged tears
reckon within the twitching of souls
Charades is not
just the game
but the poison
they drink daily
They laid drunk
in the center of the bed
photographing plastic memories

Love was just a word they wanted to believe

Crying Romance

She craves
his soft touch
She misses
the scent of the candle
and the slow dance
She's often
wondered what disappeared
over many years
She misses
the attention
and the engaging conversations
She misses
his animalistic desire
She misses
the romance and
it's been crying for decades
She longs
for his loving kiss
She misses
his sensitive warmth
She aches
for completeness
She cries
out for balance and equality
She has watched
that gap of distance grow
Romance is crying

Twisted Fairy Tales

Lovesick and in a thousand
bits of agony spread out over the dust
Shredded and defeated
No golden paths or marble dance floor
The wrecking disco ball evaporated
Romeo was convicted of manslaughter
and wearing bell bottom jeans
Aimlessly driving through quicksand
Drowning in pity and tossing
the words of Shakespeare into the trash
Juliet stood frozen on the center stage
manipulating the script in her mind
No longer believing in the crystal ball
love becoming a nightmare not a fairytale
The poets and songwriters' clench to
melodies of sarcasm and emptiness

A Crack in the Lullaby

And the chimes on the porch
whistle to the roar
And the faucet drips a lonely
drop of sorrow into the sink
And the stairs have a thin
board to make a crying melody
And the fools in the bed
sleep beside plastic hearts
And the rusty garbage can
rattles off anticlimactic jokes
And the couch has been
reminiscing of the teenage years
And the doorknobs in the hall
sob from the ageless slams
And the coffee cups fight
over glazed donuts and cinnamon toast
And the glasses of water
seek optimism in the dark
And the comic books
in the dresser drawer salivate next
to the X Rated magazines
And the mobile in the crib
has a crack in the lullaby
And the lock on the door plays
the piano to emptiness

Spite and Residue

Between the depths of the lies and
the shadows of the truth crawls
lives the slippery residue

Love is dangling
Love is slipping
Love is shrieking

Between the purple dying leaves and
the raging trunk of the dying tree shines
lives the river of freedom

Love is morbid
Love is a sour taste
Love is hollow

Between the shallow creek of anger and
the footsteps of carelessness live
the adverse corridor

Love is fading
Love is a haze
Love is blurry

Between the reckless conversations and
the spite of silence is the fear on the front page

Love is nonexistent
Love is disappearing
Love is callous

Dark Love Song

Pomegranate bruises
Accepting degradation
Spirit blackballed
Thirsty for affection
Burned out from begging
Draining self-worth
Exasperated blood
Dog tired of beatings
Fatigued of loneliness
Nauseated and disheartened
In a dark love song

Blood Paint

She sketched me
a biting breezes
I brushed a stroke
of blood paint
on her wounded knee
She fell into the pit
of the abstract skies
As I sat in purgatory
playing the iron fiddle
She hurdled the
flashing disturbance
As I held on to her
ancient pieces
I saw her tired eyes
blink for a millisecond
The gore continued

Bleeding Sea of Anguish

Beneath the crooked moon
Faded colors of lost memories are buried
Solitude warfare and emptiness were
lying on the wretched beach
The bleeding sea of anguish
fills the torn heart
Indifference has been a treacherous band aid
Destiny was never a welcome mat
Nor was the twist of fate in my palm
Love is just the wind that
scratches my face but can't grip
Your presence has evaporated
Nothing about you echoed in your disappearance

Tragic Painting

Crawl inside the decorated masterpiece
Crawl in the garden of this hollow fairytale
Crawl in the trenches to gasp for air
Crawl inside this lost graveyard
Crawl inside this wound of romance
Crawl in the river between anger and hate
Crawl in the carnival to laugh at despair
Crawl inside this forgotten casket
Crawl inside this broken melody
Crawl in the words of this pale chapter
Crawl in the tainted memories
Crawl inside this tragedy without a trace

As Her Mascara Runs

The silver bracelet falls
on the crooked pavement as her mascara runs
Her bedazzled mindset sits in an empty jar
Her pockets are empty as she fumbles for the keys
His presence consumed her existence
He stood as a curse with deranged tattoos
She is entwined in failure mediocrity
and her bones are as fragile as her captive heart
She raised the white flag but clearly
he didn't recognize her surrender
The discomfort and turmoil scatters through her veins
The ache and lost flame disappeared in their youth
She has outgrown his lack of maturity
She drove away recognizing to move forward was to let go

The Widow's Photographs

Staring into a bronze reflection
A ray of a silver lining was reborn
Reminiscing of the constants
As the variables float like rafts
Ribbons and badges decolorize
Glancing at still memories
Sharpen edges stir the mind
Gnawing and clawing at the drops
of paint rapture her soft heart
Fixated at the scenery from
an antique rocking chair
Cherishing the moments that
they created for a lifetime
Capturing the tenderness of
his hands melt away the pain

Rolling Tears

Adrenaline rushes
as I hold your head
Watching your
innocence
Anguish builds up
Rolling tears
Loving you
completely
Willing to
do anything
for you
Rolling tears
shared blood
praying you
are okay
Realizing I
have a
precious gift
Rolling tears
are present
because you
are my center

Sucker Punched

I've been walloped by your butterfly mask
I've been bashed by your holy art thou wisdom
I've been slammed by your sinful justifications
I've been battered in this emotional slugfest
I've been belted by your catatonic stare
I've been jabbed by your staggering intellect
I've been drilled by your spilled ink
I've been pulverized by the word you use called "love"
I've been beaten down to the bottom of this angry cell

If I Had Known

If I had known
her heart was so delicate
I would have been gentle

If I had known
that I was immature
I would have been patient

If I had known
she would have changed
I would have stayed

If I had known
she would take her own life
I would have done things differently

If I had known
this would have changed me forever
I wouldn't have done anything different

Bone Chilling Truth

Wrapped up in the disappointment
the bone chilling truth
Constantly devouring vanilla
Uneventful and predictable
Advertised yourself in a satin red
Underneath was plaid and stripes
Simplicity and mediocrity
Becoming comfortable and boring
Tuning the conversations out
Aiming for the ribbon and status

Paralyzed Wings

Up against the
threshold
Stolen pieces
of the sun
tear my flesh
Broken mirrors
are below my
restless feet
Careless words
are spoken
My efforts
are not enough
Sacrifices
are made not
for me
But for the
grand image
you can't see
I no longer
feel valued
and appreciated
All I feel are my
paralyzed wings
As time surpasses
you forget the
foundation we built

Bottle of Ink

Your name smudged
And your lies smeared to the edges
Your autograph disappears
And your prejudice spills all over
Your sentiments glare
And your irrelevant opinions puke
Your stance stalks in the hours
And your posture wrinkles
Your expressions digress
And your presence strips as a whore
Your observations spread
And your bottle of ink diffuses
Your ignorance blinked
And your honesty bailed
Your plastic mindset cracked
And your words are meaningless

Ocean of Tears

I begged and pleaded
for her twinkling attention
I begged and pleaded
for her words to never end
I begged and pleaded
for her lies to be swept under the rug
I begged and pleaded
for her anxiety brought to light
I begged and pleaded
for her kindness to be authentic
I begged and pleaded
for her kindred spirit to glow
I begged and pleaded
for her love to be real
I begged and pleaded
that my tears would not create an ocean

Stain in the Jaundice Eye

Envy unravels
Stain in the jaundiced eye
Insecurity is a fury sun
Losing logical abilities
Rationality is ridiculous
Hovering and protective
of what is already yours
Possessing little faith
in your beloved spouse
Jealousy is a dark shade
of green that pushes
Demoralizes relationships
Breaks into pieces
All because of your blurry
Self-serving perception
You will lose what you
thought you were
clinging to like a blanket
Swallow that

Gust of Clarity

Forgive me for my toxic sins
Forgive me for my selfish castles
Forgive me for my blind eyes
Forgive me for inhaling indifference
Thank you for lending a hand

Forgive me for dancing with fire
Forgive me for staring at my wounds
Forgive me for sleeping with my sorrow
Forgive me for my distortions
Thank you for touching my hand

Forgive me for building walls
Forgive me for igniting storms
Forgive me for my stumbling fortress
Forgive me for my thickening distress
Thank you for holding my hand

Ballistic Eyes

Ballistic eyes
Above my winter ocean
Evaporated paragraphs
crawl in the pitch black
Wearing anxiety
like a choking scarf
Cementing loneliness
contemplating a purpose
Examining unfulfilled
desires and needs
Read the divorce papers

Dismal Fool

I saw a glimpse of
your 10,000-pound chain around your neck
I saw a shadow of
your innocence mangled in the light
I saw the four corners of
your fractured mind bend for others
I saw a building of
your screaming echo crumble to my feet
I saw the fool of
myself in your precious mirror
I saw the faith of
my existence shine for the first time
I saw the world of
endangered light disappears in my tears
I saw the real you
magnify under a microscope

Waltzing into Shock

No longer do I waltz into shock
She wears laziness like a scarf
Stuffing struggles in a suitcase
Lacking the inner strength
A thin and weak vocabulary
Seeking nonexistent air
Forming a fog like perception
Cutting the rope of clarity
Standing still in the earthquake
No longer am I flabbergasted
The perplexity has diminished
She lives in the frozen movement

Engraved Clouds

Viscous air rises
Compressed aspirations
Notions within the commotion
Fraudulent impressions
Sculptured tear drops
Revolving around reflection
Completely bruised
Overshadowed tenderness
Scattered within the shattered
Sensitivity whittled
Chiseled affection
Picking up the pieces
Memorizing engraved clouds

Terrorizing Razor

A Goddess among queens
Fearful and destructive
Volcanic eruptions
A conniving manipulator
Overbearing and hostile
Seductive chains
A bewitching dictator
Terrorizing razor
Lethal injections
A deceitful treacherous woman
Hellacious and ruling
Ruthless vixen
A circling blood clot in her veins
Former lover

Forsaken Teardrops

I relapsed in your stratosphere
I took a nosedive in your heartache
I tumble in your crying shadows
I subside in the sterile danger
Your love was poison

I sink in your liquid fragility
I was plummeting in your overcast
I stepped on to your somber path
I ignored your fake complexion
Your love was forsaken

I abandoned your midnight kiss
I ran away from your dying obscurity
I feared your blistered scars
I shook my head to your revelations
Your love was torture

Glitter and Tinsel

You threw
the glitter and tinsel at my mouth
You threw
compliments I knew would fade
You threw
words without a sound
You threw
a playbook I already read
You threw
colors of paint I already touched
You threw
lights around my sensitive neck
You threw
a shard of glass at my eyes
You threw
glitter and tinsel that I knew would
eventually fall to the ground

A Prison's Shadow

Scattered thunder
Crawling sprinkles
Fixated at the hemorrhage
Convulsing shocks
Excruciating drops of sadness
A stench of torment
Fading sentiments
Evaporating warmth
A crescendo of animosity
Disgusted frown
Love is just a shadow in a prison

Slowly

Slowly
I am beginning to resent you
Slowly
I can see that I was right
Slowly
I can recognize you don't have the strength
Slowly
I can see what you didn't hear
Slowly
I am seeing what I expected to happen
Slowly
I can see I hated being right
Slowly
I tried to give you the warnings
Slowly
I gave you everything you could want
Slowly
I am becoming ignored
Slowly
It shows you were not prepared

Careless

You may have thought
you stepped on dirt
But truthfully you stepped
into mud because
you couldn't see me
I thought I saw a
bouquet of marigolds
But truthfully, I saw
Orange blossoms because
I couldn't see you
Let's face it
We couldn't see each other

Empty Discussions

Underline the word love
Find its significance
Absorb its emphasis
I'm not allowed to
convey with my tongue
But only my heart
Struggling between
physical and emotional love
Overpowering sensations
pierce me
Gushing rivers flow through
my erotic mind
Trying to find the meaning
of long-lasting love
in this empty discussion

Undertow of Chaos

Turning the mystical corner
Shedding a lonely cloak
Stumbling into an undertow
of trembling chaos
Cutting the vine of trust
Assuming the worst of me
makes me never
want to touch you
Presuming danger and harm
But continually using
words you don't mean
Accepting loneliness
as a shade of grey
Understanding I've been

The Raven's Poison

Once upon a midnight fear
she took a sip of corrosion
Debilitating mannerisms and quirks
fumbling through a frenzy
Gliding inside hallucinations
staggering outside the commotions
A recollection of mourning

Stern exchanges melting
comments and remarks growl
Sentiments dressed in black
treasures whispering hush
ripping dead skin with caution
crumbling faith turns into dirt
A recollection of mourning

Hunger flexing with animosity
Greed pointing with saliva
In holy matrimony with the raven
She tasted the hollow bitterness
Numb and disgusted by the poison
Infuriated with the toxic rants
A recollection of mourning

Provoked by exasperation
Anxiety wrapped around her neck
Choking on sour corruption
Addicted to the murmurs
Inhaling by a malicious tongue
A recollection of mourning

A catastrophic touch bellowed
Infatuation hung as a disaster
Benevolence was a chewed-up dog bone
Loneliness exhaled rapidly
Sympathy was an old rag
Love was just mucus from a cough
A recollection of mourning

SIPPING SELF DESTRUCTION

"Self-destruction is blind and blurry."

Black Vodka

The moonlight is desensitized rom the black vodka
She is drunk from the laughing skeletons in her closet
She cringes to opening the frozen door

Spinning rooms
Tarantulas crawl
Reckless she falls

She drinks the poison that soothes her emptiness
The ink from the pen that drips into her diary
Is intoxicated from her loneliness
The light that she seeks is miles away from the tunnel

Fears do bleed
Inebriated from anger
Blindness is all she can see

She drowns in the bottle of sorrow
She denies the wind of change
She would rather stay in turmoil and dwell

Alcoholic Diaries

She woke up to the sound of thumping
The sound magnified and gave her goose bumps
She laid there in distress and every movement
felt like she was being trampled
Her eyelids felt like dumbbells
The blazing sun that beamed through the window
hollered at her flesh
That smell of sizzling bacon and yellow submarine eggs
made her make a lizard face
The night before was all a blur, drinking mountains of alcohol
to erase the pain
Her memory is slowly becoming black
The twinkle disappeared in her serene eyes
The smile has turned into a catatonic frown
The ground beneath her stumbling feet
is beginning to deteriorate
The blue skies are now witchcraft gray
with a splash of alcohol
dripping from the tormented stars
She doesn't even look up anymore
She can only see the bottom
of a glass and slurs her drunken words

Rattlesnake Postcard

A restless strawberry blonde
is posing for a pickup line
The lipstick reeked desperate
measures to fill an empty void
The nicotine is vile
as the band is warming up
by playing the Allman Brothers
Charlie stumbles in through the door
cursing his ex-wife's name
The bartender chuckles
as he is pouring shots of Jack Daniels for
the bachelor partying in the corner
The conversations feel dyslexic
as the customers become trashed and plastered
Some are trying to find the answers
at the bottom of a glass
Some are trying to celebrate a victory
milestone or wash away the hollow shell
Amanda never talks to strangers
unless she has a beer in her hand
Jackson is patiently waiting
to make a transaction with Charlie
This is the place or a midnight rendezvous
The kegs are slowly disappearing
The bottles are empty just like the customers
that walk into the "Rattlesnake"
I was just reading the postcard
from Charlie and things haven't change

Under a Bloodshot Moon

Between the blackouts and the vertigo
Slurred discussions evaporate in the smog
Excuses and cursed words creep in
Empty words reside at the bottom

Even the bloodshot moon cries

Between the collision and the stars
Sound of the gin on the rocks washes away
Sarcasm and coughed up memories
Acceptance of losses linger in the cold

Even the bloodshot moon cries

Between the anger and the doubt
Brick walls rise inside my head
Drowning in the misery and sadness
Reveling in the toxic moment

Even the bloodshot moon cries

Between the strangers and ignorance
Conversations vibrate and tremble
Loneliness staggers among the silence
Bottled up screams whisper

Even the bloodshot moon cries

Inebriated Weather Report

There is a light chance
of vodka on the rocks
I can see the precipitation
of Jim Beam and coke
There will be a blizzard
of Sam Adams and Guinness
I can feel the storm
of Gin and Tonic
Out west there is a blazing ray
of Long Island Ice Teas
Up north throughout the week
You will taste Bloody Marys
By the end your head will spin
and pass out due to consumption

Sinister Winds

Fermented colloquy
A sharp taste on my tongue
Pungent and rancid
Curdling dialogue
Stepping into your jagged tone
Defeating and morbid
A deafening acidic side splitter
Translations camouflaged
Apocalyptic exclaim
Walking off the stumbling buzz
Torn from an emotional brawl
Sentenced to a disturbance
Derailed from sinister winds

A Curved Hook (Parasites Drinking Tears)

Constantly scrutinized
Consistently criticized
A fragile shadow gazes
Comparatively obtrusive
Condescendingly obtuse
A curved hook gravitates
Constructing nailed crossroads
Constricting scrambled oxygen
A war within the veins ascends
Confined territories of tears
Condemned mirrors
A theatre of parasites descends

Out of Order

Dressed in contradictions
Sleeps with agitations
Naked in confrontations
Torn with separation
Masked in addictions
Consumed with friction
Sidetracked in hesitations
Withdrawn with preservation
Falling in hallucinations
Defeated with aberrations
Sandblasted in quicksand
Blown with devastation

Clawing and Grinding

Clasping to the vicious sound
Grinding my teeth to loneliness
Clenching to the hollow rattle
Snagging the callous pages
Latching on to the emptiness
Seeking the comfort in the corner
Clutching to the invisible truth
Absorbing the bitterness
Digesting too much judgement
Consuming bits of the view
Seizing the blankness
Clawing inside my cage
Refusing to listen and understand
where I was and where I am

Bottle of Shadows

Leave me a pile of scrutiny
Leave me a bag of aggravation
And I will toss it in the dying closet

Leave me a tiny bit of solitude
Leave me an ounce of spoiled milk
And I will throw it in the empty pantry

Leave me a gallon of spiked juice
Leave me a shred of laughter
And I will painfully swallow the bits

Leave me a bottle of shadows
Leave me a jug of sarcasm
And I will watch myself drown

Leave me a tank of affliction
Leave me a plate of dirty lies
And I will break another mirror

Leave me a pair of worn out glasses
Leave me a little bit of rust
And I will never see my heart ache

Aggravated Core

Decimated to bits
Exterminated to slices
Destroyed by snakeskin claws
Leveled by blackness
Obliterated to kingdom come
A numb aggravated core
Loneliness is suicide
Inside destruction
Dismantled and ripped
Erased from existence
Tensions no longer scream
Silence and flat line entwine
Goodbye

Ripped Chill

At the end of the coarse rope
At the end of the thin line
At the end of a dead-end mindless street
At the end of the distant seizure
At the end of the waking chill
At the end of the chaotic silence
At the end of the endless liquid
At the end of the ripped vocal cord
At the end of the bloodstream
At the end of the terrorizing nightmare

Growl from the Wall

In silence the moans crawled like graffiti from the wall
In wailing thunder the anger was deafening
In the grumble she arched her red tip wings
In the rolling her halo disappeared in the rapture
She snarled at the first of December
She fell into the roar of the winter shackle
In the yell she crudely despised the minutia
She whispered to the autumn kiss
She bellyached over torn dialogue
In the complaining she swallowed the past
She criticized the truth as it gulped her like alcohol

Cloud of Dust

I sat in a puddle of insignificance
I stand in sand of irrelevance
I am undistinguished to you
I posed in a senseless portrait
I fell in a pointless discussion
I am minor in your grand vision
I sink in a vapor of nothing
I find myself alone in conversations
I am a cloud of dust in your clarity

Scent of Emptiness

Pulled heart strings
Recorded whispers at a dead-end street
Telephone wires ripped
And Velcro tattered wings fall

Lashing of a dangerous tongue
Transfusions of vertigo
Neon needles lit on the graveyard shift
And deafening beats of solitude cry

Pockets full of copper
Choking scrambled poison
Trails of blood money at my feet
And the silver spoon cracks

Convicted of breaking veins
Stealing the scent of perfume
Intimidating romance
And I raise the glass to loneliness

Dressed for traveler's checks
Leaving for cards and dice
Guzzling a cup of burgundy
And I toast to the shell of myself

Rattle in a Cage

Indecisions hide like bats in the echoes of the cave
Uncertainty sips from the acidic river
Vinegar seeping between the crushed bones and sharp nerves
Isolation and desolation are thumbs ripped from each hand
And the rattle lingers in the corner of the ear drum
Dismay is tucked away behind a faded curtain
Flaws stick to me like starving fleas
Substance is the saliva dripping from the piranha's teeth
The equilibrium inside me wakes up the storm
And the rattle parades in a rhythm that disturbs the haze
Symptoms of a nontransparent disease spread
Inside the soliloquy the cage embraces the thunder
Murmurs and grumbles tremble with fright
Theology and myths walking in unison
And the rattle pounds like a headache
Butchered insults and splinters drive three inches through my anger
Crude laughs and vicious skies open up pouring sadness
Exasperation drags my eyelids through the dirt
Sorrow is a creek that I cleanse the silence
And the rattle pierces my aching skin
And I lay here with the rattle in the cage soothing the emptiness

Beneath the Ruthless Sun

Dried out perceptions lay still
Recycled stories aren't read
Penning the same old story
Repetitiveness is revolving
As you fail to evolve
Beneath the ruthless sun
Seeking sound in the silence
Ignoring the heartbeat of self- love
Hoping for others to see
Your worth and beauty
Quit praying for the rain
Stop praying for the storm
Crawl like millions
And change the scenery
Only the ruthless sun
Will make you blind

Empty Casket

I've stared at my casket
I've stared at what you don't want
I've stared at my doubts
I've stared at what you ignored
I've stared at my beliefs
I've stared at what you throw away
I've stared at my reflection
I've stared at what you don't do
I've stared at my fears
I've stared at what you don't want
I've stared at my existence
I've stared at the thought of not being here

Falling Stigma

Falling slowly
I'm a walking stigma
A human disorder
Deflated and lonely
Drifting sideways
I'm a ruptured phantom
A discolored malfunction
Frayed and distant
Losing ground
I'm a jagged knife
A pale memory
Torn and distraught
Unforgiven tattoo
I'm a black enigma
A missing piece
Empty and hollow

Tumultuous Scar

She woke up
fragilely disheartened
Stumbling through
the vacant parking lots
She feared the poison
but chose to swallow
the disturbance
She is helplessly frozen
by the enigma
Falling through
the suffocating blurs
She stretches
her cauterized reflection
Desperately seeking
self-preservation
She covers her
tumultuous scar
with black mascara
to ignore the recklessness

Suicide's Wrath

Below the forbidden
atmosphere
Your venomous instincts
blink in your ferocious eyes
Naturally unfeeling
Detecting your malevolent
and atrocious voice
Watching you evolve
becoming a degenerate
Casting judgments
As if you were a bronze standard
inhaling your charcoal and
sipping on toxic sauce
Hallucinations of blood
dripping from your pale neck
As you lay frozen in blue
Self-destruction was
your rotten charm
leaving an innocent child behind
As I carry the weight
on my broad shoulders
My sensitivity turns into stone
watching the bricks stack
Your funeral lurks in
the shadows of my mind
Infuriated with the outcome

Two Headed Monster

Jealousy is a two
headed monster
that can't see its
color of ugliness
Dressed up in
stubbornness
and obsession
I tried to speak
to it calmly and
with compassion
But the two headed
monster didn't
have any ears and
refused to listen
The monster walked
away on its own

Silence Kills

The walls of courage
have disintegrated
Nothing about her emotions and
thoughts are emancipated
She is the only one
that can bare the bottled truth
The word rape
is etched to her bleeding heart

Scream
Cry
Bellow
Silence kills
Please try to speak
You are the victim

The bruises and pain
are a distorted color of agony
She would give anything
to erase the memory
Nothing can ease
her shame and wounds
The word blame
is sewn to her chest

Scream
Tear up
Bellow
Silence kills
Please try to speak
You are the victim
Free yourself

Drops of Anguish

Snowflakes disappear
Drops of anguish bellow
Leaves twirl innocently
Frustrations become frail
Black rain dissolves
Woven remembrance
Cemented sorrow
Etched Fragrance
Capturing the light
Closed chapters
Relinquished clouds
Bottled thoughts
Beloved distress
No goodbyes

Embedded Stain

I've tried
to wash off the salt from my wounds
I've tried
to walk on the sand barefoot
I've tried
to walk off the crippling pain
I've tried
to walk on the edge of my reality
I've tried
to walk off the circling buzz
I've tried
to walk on my monumental mistakes
I've tried
to walk off my stumbling ignorance
I've tried
to walk on the road to peace
I've tried
to walk off the forgiveness
But I can't
I can't seem to look at me

Digesting Self Destruction

I've tried to digest you
But I can't even with a
chugging of a good beer
Too large of a pill
I've tried to understand
as the compassion
sits at the steel brim
Too self-destructive
As you are so unaware
Fantasy expectations
Never hearing yourself
speak out loud
I never judge or point
Too many complications
Due to your lack
of understanding your
pieces of reality that
you refuse to look at

Silently Incarcerated

In a faded brick dungeon
Goodbye written in cursive
on the comatose barricade
Silently incarcerated for
not forgiving myself
Staring at the inner shadows
Paralyzed by the fears
Hibernating from the
distant accusations
Collapsing to the ground
from the violent prosecution
Lies refusing to evaporate
Evidence held hostage
Deserving to be in contempt
Verdict closing in on
my prisoned and deranged soul
Swallowing the key

Stubborn Key

Locked away
in a stormy diluted vault
Wreckage of trees
Pile of disguises
Human damage
Protecting inner self
Disregarding others
Living for one
Absorbed in exile
Speechless and afraid
No quest for growth
No search for evolution
The stubborn key
is in your clammy palm

Tasting Resentment

Acidic and tart
Constantly coughing
Failing and falling
Replaying scenes
Blind should haves
Ignored could haves
Struck by reality
Trapped by the outcome
Forcing the mind to bend
Still constantly choking
Tasting resentment

Cursed Diamond

Sulking in the leather booth
She sips on her vodka on the rocks
The mascara is running due to her kaleidoscope tears
She is staring down at her notepad
drawing hearts around the deceased name
Often, she struggles displaying emotions and genuine affection
She was born to be a stone
The melancholy around her knife shaped soul
swarms the emptiness
She looks at herself as if she is a cursed diamond
She is surrounded by greed, politicians, clowns and thieves
Excuse me, aren't they all the same thing?
The wealth she accumulated over the years were other's misfortunes
She has worn the best fake smile as the years have faded
She has aged gracefully but her withered heart has been in a life
size pinball machine
As she has sat there staring at the notepad the reality
shook her foundation
She will leave this earth without her possessions
The smoke in the air continues to thicken

Hopelessly Drowning

I caress your benevolence
I caress your chained insecurities
I caress your shards of the moon
I'm craving your fragrance
I caress your stimulation
I caress your trusting mind
I caress your value of a dollar
I have an overwhelming desire
I caress your fallen tears
I caress your blanket covering your stitches
I caress your overflowing soul
I'm sleepless in your dreams
I caress your supple skin
I caress your endowing heart
I caress your fingertips
I'm hopelessly drowning in you

Bottomless Crutch

Pouring down overused mentalities
Change fumbling around
Pulling four quarters to insert
in the old-fashioned jukebox
Numbers exchanged between
the mentalist and the statue
Between the shot glass
and the pint of an Irish stout
Scattered observations are slurred
Tiptoeing through the cigar vapors
and the barking stilettos
Polluted with aggravation
and lipstick smudges on the glass
Empty barstools are playing violins
Loneliness waits for no one
Be careful where you drown
your heartache and sorrows
Look up at the glaring neon sign
The Bottomless Crutch

DRENCHED IN RAGE

"Anger is the most dangerous enemy."

The Devil's Blacklist

Even the Devil himself chuckles
The moon is carved with your lies
Tangled up in your demented mind
Serenaded by demonic gargoyles
Stains of convoluted fairytales twitch
Nightmares glide through your skull
As you become the twisted spin doctor
Even the Devil himself despises you
The haunted tree is covered in your sins
Using the phrase "Sick and dying" to draw attention
The line for the roller coaster to hell banishes the disturbed and psychopathic rants
Even the Devil himself cringes at your name
Fearing your chameleon sadistic skin
Wallowing in your fragile bones
Be careful what you curve with your tongue

The Empty Star Named Desiree

She offered me an overcoat of affection
laced in demented lies
She slipped me a blank check
with her Chinese lipstick imprint of her thin line lips
She surrounded me with a magician with a limp
pianist with eight fingers and a dyslexic author
She is regarded as the empty star named Desiree
She discarded me as a broken tooth
She glided around me as a soulless gypsy
She wore her agendas underneath her crown of deceit
She offered me illusions of comfort dressed in daggers
cutting into my mirror
She left chards of glass on the floor with speckles of dust
She was mesmerized by the decaying memory of her birth
She appealed to my sense of wonder
She catapulted my scattered dreams in a box and sealed it shut
She was a transparent disease with a belligerent tongue
She scolded my sincerity with her toxic scent
She detested my ray of light and any shred of my dignity
She can slither back into that empty star and disappear

Twitching Carnival

She blooms to carve out her destiny
She seeks out what appears does not exist
The reflection in the mirror is the dark outline of the chaos
inside the unicorn
The illusions are compromised with bitterness and what can never be
She twitches to the sound of reality
This no longer feels like love
She was born to be bright as the white sand
She is no longer a hidden gem
a discovered moon stones
The carnival in her mind dribbles
She crawls away out of confidence
She deserves more than what has been given
The shell she cracked is in pieces of stolen memories
She no longer borrows laughter
The carnival inside her mind has stiches
The bleeding stops here
The words are empty
It no longer feels real

Skin of the Beast

I shivered feeling your wrath
I was quivering from the force of your leather hand
I was stone cold frozen from your dominant words
You make my blood cold
and my bones brittle
The hatred boiled
as the hand of the clock barely moved
I was bitten
from the skin of the beast
You were more dangerous
than a python wrapped around my throat
You were more corrupt
than a devious politician
I was smashed to smithereens
and smothered from your vile tongue
I loathed your wretched touch
and cringed to your voice

Coughing Up a Smirk

A damp scowl tickles her throat
Sly and slippery as ice
A sour taste in her mouth
Vengeance and venom slide
down like an infant's snot
A smug and deranged gleam
The smirk ricochets off
the bullets from her forehead
A bark and a buzz splatter
Retribution and vindication hobble
Coughing up a sugar-coated lie
stains and glares
Tooth and nails scratch at the core
Never underestimate her wrath

Dramatic Trash

Stirred up conversations
Communication breakdown
Misinterpreted and misconstrued
Temperatures flaring
Over exhausted, boiling points
Tired and restless
from your toxic mouth
Carefully choosing
every word
Walking on already
cracked eggshells
Please hit
the repeat button
Dialogue spinning
in wide circles
Trash piling up
from your drama
Nobody can hear
your run-on sentences
Diluted paraphrasing
and ridiculousness
Deciding to not
reply to your ignorance
Choosing to walk away
from an adult
Realizing mentally
you are a child

Sour Moon

Diabolical nerves
crawling hemorrhage
Conniving gloom
Dying underneath a sour moon
Stroking a clawing ego
Cloaked in agendas and lust
Walking transparent
Swallowing my spit
Leaking semen
Rated X photographs
Blackmail and fraud
Knives turning and twisting

Walking Infection

Pathetic poison
Society's outcast
Thoughtless and insensitive
Spineless serpent
Southern dirt
A pile of excrement
Frozen and acidic
A world cancer
An eye sore
Liquid evil
Pure contamination
Like a kidney stone
Rotten to the center
You are rejected
from the mass
Manipulative and sinister
A Stephen King character
A world class stalker
You are an infection

Riot Poison

Dysfunctional chaos
boils around her cerebral brain
collecting useless trivial knowledge
bouncing around in her shell

Magnetized to other misfortunes
corrosion settling in her veins
Sipping sour riot poison
to soothe her boxed up pain

Sadistic bliss is scalding her
tremors and trampled dandelions
fragile bones turn to rust
seas burning in her violent eyes

Intangibles becoming cauterized
manipulation is her best friend
Unable to feel the loneliness
despite the thorns in her back

Valentine Sin

To breathe in your ego
To gasp at your might
To appreciating you as a human
To absorbing your words
To no longer respecting you
To just appeal to your language
To see you are a sin
To claim your title as a bitch
To see you are conceited
To not notice my words

Psychobabble

Psychobabble is drooling
Filth sliding off your tongue
To a world that doesn't want you
Chaotic rambles spill
Flourishing idiotic sentences
To only a southern cult following
Despised and detested
The walking antichrist
An asylum meant for your family
Raising children to scream
Not speaking with an ounce of intelligence
Your mother should have used a condom
So, the world didn't have to put up with
Your nonsense and illogical thoughts

Aneurysm

Vessels stretching
Anger swims violently
Down pouring angst
Collisions of hatred
Twitching skin
Flooded with sweat
Discombobulated fluids
Repulsed by your stains
Disturbing cries of lust
covered in cancer
High pitch shrieks
Revolting yells of help
Lay there catatonically
Photograph my smirk

Expiration Date

Incurable senseless fraud
Nauseas from your small
dying vocabulary
A grotesque fake villain
Over exhausted stupidity
Revolting and skeletal
Worthless devious stain
Infectious and squeamish
A pale rotten tumor
Patiently waiting for you
to drown in your dust
On the edge of absurdity
for your expiration date
Your remains evaporate
Silence is glorious
Lacking tolerance of
your wasted space

Dog's Rattling Jaw

Rippling chatterbox
A tongue of a cult minister
Wretched salivating beast
Shoving beliefs down
your raw throat with a
diamond skull pitchfork
Monstrous tattletale
Never ending movements
of her blood thirsty lips
Cunning rabid wolverine
clawing at your character
shoveling fertilizer in
her rattling horrid crevice
Anxiety heightens as her
head is yanked as I stare
into her black hole eyes
with my soft pale smirk

Laceration King

In the land of aggravation
Anguish and discomfort blister
Cold distress reverberates
Excruciating affection bubbles
from the flamethrower of agony
Jewelry from the laceration king
illuminates among the irritations
Wounds from the torture
glisten and throb throughout
the reckless shivering nights
The queen of devastation blinks
Trembling conversations shudder
Laughter spasms and drools
Faith wiggles and squirms
throughout the crumbled dirt
Love fidgets in the clouds and trees
under a pitch-black sky

The Savage's Ace

Incoherently bursting
Drawing the last card from
the ancient deck
Eyeballing the translucent
phantasm glaring at me
Magnetically being pulled
into the ace of the savage
Tiptoeing into the tangled
weeds of the numb circus
Dragged into a technicolor
hellacious sphere
Secret garden weep
Chameleons dressed in
treasured costumes
Branches swaying to the
sound of a smooth saxophone
Wildcats wrestling with
diabolical wisecracks
Rivers of alcohol surrounding
a gust of melancholy mirages
Anacondas smirking
Prancing with the windstorm
Guiding me back into
the ace of the savage
Thrusting forward to see
a shadow of realism

Wrath of the Circus

The bellowing trumpets, flying roses, and children's laughter spill out in the banana parade
Ladies and gentlemen people of all ages let me embrace you with our mythological circus
The soulless acrobat without a vein walks a tightrope
The troubled trapeze artist steals the show with his limping courage
The drunken clown dazzles many with her sensual walk
The smell of popcorn, cotton candy clouds, and fountains of syrup are in front of your nostrils
The strongest man is weakened by the lack of attention
The flickering lights rage over the roar of the crowd
The juggler is balancing his demons and forgotten joys
The tiger isn't tamed by his master but by the cage the audience constructed
The vultures, ravens, and lovebirds lose their feathers in this affair of the entertainment
Your senses will be heightened, and realities will vanish for a three-hour show
Step inside the monsoon and feel the wrath of the apocalyptical circus

The Skeleton's Magic

From the marrow
of your bleached bones
I gawk at your cloudy view

From the vessels
of your decaying brain
I peek at your vile lungs

From the ivory skin
to your numb heart
I overlook your flaws

From the incubus
of your wretched soul
I gaze into your core

From the veins
of your savage truth
to your circus tales

I scan the turbulence
of your existence
I rejoice in seeing
the skeleton's magic

Leaking Disarray

Walking terror
A needling headache
Laced in crime
Spiked high heels
Swallowing animalism
Tied to manipulate
Unorthodox perception
Raping the innocent
Unconventional suction
Wearing a collar of deceit
Chained to flames
Licking the drippings
Genuine leaking disarray

The Night Crawler

Your emotions touch me like a night crawler
Your erratic thoughts sit still in each corner of the room
Deep into the forest
You seek me like a stalker
Your words are overwhelming, and the comfort is troubling
Your happiness is too dependent on my accomplishments
Deep into the night
Your perception is your reality
Your needs are becoming sticky fingers
Your world has my outlines that I didn't draw with a pen
Deep into the cold
You disregard that my thoughts are frozen

Poisonous Earwax

Displeased with the disposition
Au revoir to your fake backbone
Standing vigorously ten feet tall
Apologetic for my identity
Walking into a depleted tone
Lacking the courage to be an adult
Unable to converse and debate
Watching admiration depreciate
to a faded penny
Connections pulled from the wall
Your skull full of poisonous earwax
Diagnosed with selfishness
Carrying a humongous ego
Wishing and hoping I desired you
But I don't backbite to your face
I stare truth in the wicked eyes
and release it from my fingertips

Idle Nerves

Ignorance painted on
your pathetic forehead
Twitching with ridiculous
Idle nerves
Harassing others due
to be an empty gasoline can
Lines drawn in the dirt
Stay in your tiny corner
Live that mundane escapade
Casting judgements and stones
Like you are the almighty
Who in the hell are you?
Use your idle nerves wisely
For once be productive
Perhaps you should be added
to the Devil's Blacklist
Nobody will want your
gutless and bloodless soul

Old Fishwife

Calmly detesting the muckraker
Only to hear the shrew gripe
Shaking her fleabag of a head
An infinity of grumbling
Speechless to the spine of a mongrel
Deteriorating complaints
She's barking at the tears of the moon
A chilling personality with bite
Criticizing and seeking faults
Without any constructive verbiage
Thoughtless with groans of displeasure
Walking away from the old fishwife

Tarantula Skull

Beneath your gruesome
and lecherous center
slowly moves centipedes
between your intestines
Cobwebs growing at a
miraculous rate between
your tarantula skull
The vein of the copperhead
wraps around your
slippery greedy heart
Nerves of glue are stuck
to your vindictive skin
Knowing you will burn
in hell forevermore

Gripping Oblivion

I saw the mental blankness
blink from your insomniac eyes
Tragedies spoon fed like an infant
Curse words falling from the corner
Desperate for minutes of affection
I saw the twinkling nirvana
cry like the tin man's angel
Misfortunes covering your web
Anger spiked with disaster
Hazardous sand under your feet
I saw you gripping oblivion
with your fists of delusion
Useless and trivial conversations
Spreading like high school rumors
submerged into carelessness

Stumbling Distortion

I stumbled into the dim cavern
And the shadows criticized me

I stumbled into the dying abyss
And the collision quietly chuckled

I stumbled into your fix
And the solution dissolved

I stumbled into the cynic mirror
And I hated all the distortion

I stumbled into the hollow shell
And I don't know how I get there

I stumbled into the dark side of myself
And I know there is a light

Tangled Snowflake

Blackouts pulsating
A defining jerk and clutch
Masterful stroke of an ego
Rather than to the three-inch appendage
Pulling rotting teeth like
Truth from a salesman
Nerves oscillating to a drum
Feeling like a tangled snowflake
In your cold shoulder dialogue
Raising your malevolent eyebrow
Crushing self-esteems due
to your shrinking inferiority
Realizing you are deprived
of sensitivity and kindness
It's you that withers in the pitch

Stomping in Vinegar

Tragically mundane
A monotone flat line
Whiplashed suction
Defeating purposes
Stale and obsolete
Stomping in vinegar
A tart existence
Boring as vanilla
Craving a simple life
Ignoring the puzzles
Making up the whole
Shredding my ideals
Ruining the essence

Devil's Tongue

She reigns to be sinister among the shallow
She requires depths and is waiting for your defense
She longs for the articulate and rainbow of a mind
His knees buckle to the sound of her voice

She stands to be vivacious with the insatiable curves
She will stalk you with her dismembered humor
She will dance with the Devil's tongue
His charm escapes his personality

She will haunt you with her ghosts of war
She will break your spirit with her vulgar display of insanity
She will unleash her wrath of hatred
He crawls inside of his broken shell

She will disown your white shadow
She will be the bullet that is shot through your chest
She claims to have been chained in the dungeon
He dies inside of himself

Dead Poetess

In her vacant eyes
Quietly she is alive
In her wide vocabulary
Silently she is dead
Playing with words
Like toys and trinkets
Withdrawn emotions
Rereading lines
Seeking sense and flow
Within a lost thin shell
Stepping inside her
Mammoth ego
Electric shocks soaring
Through her wretched body
My mind turns to the left
At these distinct crossroads

Frozen Verses

Transgressions overlap digressions
Watching a flawless moonlight
Disappear between lurking fear
Silence released in a murky sea
spreading like oil among the ruins
Unfastened the poetic verses
Stripping the violet language
of affection but gasping for air
Ripping controversy from your
faded and ancient wings
As you fly like the butterfly over
Icebergs dropping photographs
of forever entwined in anger
Struggling with interpretation
Rereading Cupid's rhymes
laced in numbness and removing
the quill from your stone-cold hand

Spoiled Rotten

Gulping a rancid pill
Sliding down the esophagus
After it settles and calms the spasms
I stare into the spoiled rotten hound
Giving up treasured dreams
Disregarding my points of view
Ignored wants and needs
Claiming to listen
But to only hear jumbled words
Questioning minuscule worth
Dollar signs draw your attention
As you stand there in your cashmere
You just need me in a coffin
To paint the picture in wide frames

Stupid Grin

Choking on sour grapes
Vermillion squinting eyes
Stomping in disdain
Resentful and stonewalled
Gazing at your stupid grin
Slapping your blasphemy
Pale lips turning maroon
Cloaking piles of messages
Quoting your holy beliefs
Glaring at your stupid grin
Mentally you are blackballed

Frostbite

You deliver a harsh goodbye
with a taste of frostbite
You struck a winters nerve
with no explanation
You disguise yourself
with shallow snowflakes
You hide behind your
deep cold vicious words
You walk into a blizzard
with a callous stare
You disregard the warmth
clenching to the ice
You are frostbite to the core

A Smeared Overture

A smudge of fear hangs above the black eye
She discounted the punchline
A dash in the wind smacked me hard
She smeared my name in the mud
A dispersed glimpse of the breeze fades
She persecuted me based on herself
A symphony played her shattered melody
She wore a discolored gown to the palace
A blistering sky laughed at her overture
She minimized the melody within me
A belittling spirit flown around me like a fly
She plastered her arrogance in my face
A prologue was written in her cold blood
She left the epilogue before the cynicism danced

Silent Bullseye

Furious and fuming
Upset and infuriated
And the silence roars
Up in arms and bent
Livid and frantic
And the quiet is rancid
Steamed and enraged
Disappointed and agitated
And the muteness is dismal
Provoked and exasperated
Inflamed and turbulent
And the dead air is thick
Exacerbated and wrathful
Sullen and resentful
And the muzzle is brisk

DRIPPING LUST

"Lust is an image and sensations that are temporary."

Salty Lust

In this sweet and taboo temptation
Rare and serene love making twitch
Watching love flicker like a switch
Misguided by all the sensations
Lust is driven by overblown heat
Grabbing and surrendering fire
Aching and craving raging desire
Blood rushing from head to feet
In this salty and disgusting mess
You said words you didn't mean
Forcing me to remove my dress
Watching this unfold become obscene
Here knowing you mean less
Hoping that this was all a dream

Lost Mistress

Bleached noise
Whispering static
Staring at the
surrendered candlelight
Haunting memories
engraved and etched
Wishing she was more
than the lost and distant mistress
Memorized the traced curves
Replaying a tornado
of misused conversations
Centered around a
bottle of wine and a cracked moon
Wishing she was the student
and I was the educated teacher
Captured all the pivotal moments
Absorbing the bright flashbacks
Neglecting that I was madly
in love and head over red heels
Lust ruined and broke my marrow

Unspoken Dance

Sipping on brandy
As the conversations stir like drinks
In the corner of my eye
walks a stunning beauty

Candlelit piano played with only fingertips
Glancing at her crimson dress from a distance
Nonchalantly photographing her candy lips
Thoughts of caressing her skin
flow like a river through my mind

The Mayfield jazz club oozes sensuality
dripping magic and chills of the spine
Our eyes meet for the first time
and the moment stood still

The piano is playing endlessly
as I pay the check in the clouds of smoke
The dance floor is empty as I stand in the center
Volts of passion soar through my body
waiting to just dance with the most beautiful
woman in the room

Elegance walks towards me as my hands wait
I place my hands on her waist and
feel the silk of the dress
Our lips are inches
apart waiting to connect

We move to the sound of the delicate piano
as we do not speak a word
As the jazz club empties invincible fire is burning
as we continue the unspoken dance

The radiance of her beauty is astonishing
I craved her essence and warmth
I respected and cherished every second
Instead of kissing her lips
I leaned in to place my lips on her cheek

As our bodies became closer
to the sound of the piano
I whispered in her ear
"I want to make love to you."

Sugar Fascination

I've undressed your kindness
and taste the sweet tea
I've undressed your words
and swallow your charm
I've undressed your candor
and step into your confidence
I've undressed your intellect
and fell in love with your wit
I've undressed your beliefs
and sleep with your poetry
I've undressed your receptiveness
and dance with your fire
I've undressed your sharpness
and licked your bitterness
I've undressed your magnetism
and latch on to your spell
I've undressed your enchanted eyes
and grip your mysterious soul
I've undressed your broken star
and see a magnificent galaxy

Sparks and Nectar

I miss the sound of your faith
I miss the sparks on your tongue
I miss our naked stars in the valiant sky
I miss the honey falling from your wings
I miss your silver harlequin
I miss the taste of your nectar
I miss the feeling of your curves
I miss the sweat from the tension
I miss the depth of the tunnel
I miss the blaze and wild smoke
I miss your scalding magnetism

Deleted Italian Scenes

Siren tongue lashing
Boiling altercation
Turning friction
into shocking magnetism
Slithering tensions
Desires eating away within
Locking away the voices
Ignoring the dangers
Releasing frustrations
in layers of colorful poetry
Disguised in a red arrow mask
Blood thirsty urges rise
Vigorous thumping
Awaiting to erupt
Watching Italian ice drip

Reservation in Ink

Temperature of lust equals
one hundred degrees
She is here because he
doesn't say she is sexy
He is here because she
doesn't curse in bed
Calmly signing them
drowning sin in ink
Heat strong as Arizona
Desires seeping in sheets
Caught up in attraction
Reservation in ink

Lost in Fantasy

I'm lost
in the translucent visual
I'm wrapped
too much into fantasy
I'm engaged
into what isn't happening

I'm staring
at the colors in my head
I'm laced
up in sexuality and wonder
I'm walking
through a wet and hazy dream

I'm feeling
so many hands reaching for me
I'm aching
for the sweat to never disappear
I'm ignoring
the parts to the puzzle

I'm chasing
the river next to the sunset
I'm bleeding
from the knife of reality
I'm recognizing
the shadows of emptiness

I'm wanting
what does not exist
I'm needing
the hands of wishes
I'm starving
for what others possess

I'm craving
for what I don't have
I'm stalking
the landscape in my head
I'm writing
for what is missing

Saturated Desire

I remember
when I felt your hunger
I can remember
when I felt your innocence
I remember
when I was saturated by your desire
I can remember
when I was embracing your touch
I remember
using that word love emphatically
I can remember
the dreams we shared
I remember
when the kiss made us cry
I can remember
when you were thirsty for me
I remember
being in a trance from the echoes of your love
I can remember
not letting go

Between Paradise and Ecstasy

I found a lurking vampire
in your mind
I found a forbidden ghost of reason
in your imagination
And you make me crazy
I found the chemistry between
your charming wit and voice
I found your grace underneath
your gorgeous sheets
And you make me crazy
I found sensuality in your words
and the fabric of your soul
I found a spell in your soft hands
and your priceless treasure
And you make me crazy
I found a gift in the seas of your eyes
and got lost
I found paradise in your love
and never want to leave
And you make me complete

Lady Hex

Nearsighted to the flash
Walking on voodoo eggshells
Entrancing and spellbound
Watching a jolt of fire rise
Flag of sacred witchcraft laughs
Haunting and mysterious
Inscrutable fingers waving
Saturated in hollow desire
Trickery between the satin sheets
Swindled by the delicious curves
Breathing abracadabra
Preying on your charm
Rocking back and forth
Slamming in and out
Only deception oozes and gushes
Tipping her black hat
A valiant and alluring lady hex

Tangled up in Tricks

I drank your monkeyshine from morning until dusk
I consumed your escapade until laughter had a scent
I fell into your delusions and swing danced with a one-handed conundrum
I scolded your impositions as the non-talking jester chuckled
I was swindled by your kindness and sweet fascinations
I was bamboozled until your thorns turned maroon
I was drenched from your storm of deception
I was intoxicated from your innocent wine
I was brainwashed from your diabolical treachery
I didn't mean to taste your bitter Shangri-La from your bottle of shenanigans
I swallowed my ignorance as the dull razor slit my throat
I bowed down to the queen as she placed her crown on with a smirk
I looked up speechless and disappeared into the pitch black

Crimson Queen

Raging fury
Violent hot head
High blood sugar
Suffocating ramblings
Nonsensical tone
Overtaken jealousy
Becoming idiotic
Swarming of
erotic emotions
Entangled between
lust and logic
Spoken from the
earthquake around
the delicate heart
Not knowing she
became the razor
Empress of power
Crimson Queen

Serenading Las Vegas

I'm not in love
with the flashing neon lights
I'm captivated by
your delightful exuberance
I'm not in awe
with blackjack and poker
I'm in tune
with your inviting voice
I'm not sucked into
America's largest playground
I'm enchanted
by your melodic truth
I'm not stung
by the sliver city
I'm pulled in
by your radiant mind
I'm waiting for the harmony
to serenade Las Vegas

Traces of Desire

Your desire is bulletproof
Your desire is smoldering
Your desire is fearless
Your desire is a never-ending aftershock
Your desire is vivid with brightness
Your desire is daring with truth
Your desire is a wicked machine
Your desire dances with invisible fire
Your desire is alluring in the quiet storm
Your desire shines like crystal
Your desire is blazing in the desert
Your desire is polarizing

Sprinkling Desire

I relish in the sunshine
on your magical tongue
I savor the sentiments
on your flammable lips
I admire the sweetness
from your miraculous smile
I idolize the brightness
of your strength
I am fascinated by the glow
of your heartbeat
I cherish your fingertips
and your precious touch
I honor your intellect
and your neon kindness
I am attached to your
soothing voice
I appreciate your rainbows
and the edges of your heart

Marmalade Boots

I eavesdrop on your footsteps
Carefully sighing to the sound
I'm waiting to see your marmalade boots
Gazing from your feet to your face
I keep my erotic thoughts in a vault
Mesmerizing your curves
I generously offer the world to you
Laughing at my gesture
I inhale her daisy perfume
Capturing her unforgettable words
"Your world is in my universe"

Twinkling Spotlight

I ran toward the twinkle of your moon
I ran toward the glimmer of your soul
Falling under your spell

I ran toward the gloss of your warmth
I ran toward the glare of your affection
Falling under your wings

I ran toward the dazzle of your spotlight
I ran toward the flash of your love
Falling under your magnificence

I ran toward the radiance of your glow
I ran toward the blink of your scent
Falling under your shine

Scorching Memories

She gave me a starlight moment
She gave me a captivating sensation
She gave me more than I could ever expect
She gave me a ray of sunshine
She gave me a bottle of passion to drink
She gave me a dash of spice
She gave me goosebumps from head to toe
She gave me the heat from the nectar
She gave me more than I could ever dream
She gave me a scorching photograph
She gave me the sounds of ecstasy
She gave me the needle to my addiction
She gave me more time than I anticipated
She gave me a bounce to my next few steps
She gave me a window to inhale her air
She gave me the reason to appreciate what I have

Wrap Me Up

Wrap me up in your vine
Wrap me up in your tender soul
Wrap me up in your sacred heart
Wrap me up in your gentle love
Wrap me up in your magnificence
Wrap me up in your wondrous glow
Wrap me up in your laughter
Wrap me up in your songs
Wrap me up in your kindness
Wrap me up in your forgiveness
Wrap me up in your precious eyes
Wrap me up in your pitch-black scars
Wrap me up in your wisdom
Wrap me up in your pink sky
Wrap me up in your warmth

Unprecedented Name

From the scribbled crux
to the highest point of sensations
your name clears my throat
Vast skin tingles and thirst growls
Oceans of lust gurgle
your name silences the storm
From your intellect and strength
to your brilliant essence
your entirety is astonishing
Stunning and remarkable
A decade of beauty
Thought to be fictitious
your name is unprecedented

PRECIOUS LOVE

"Every shade of love is beautiful."

Falling for a Sunrise

I'm falling
for a sunrise that
ignites a magical flame

I'm falling
for the brightness
of her scars

I'm falling
for her
enigmatic strength

I'm falling
for her truth
humanity and her genuine heart

I'm falling
for a sunrise that
shines so bright

I'm not afraid
of falling
I just fear
the height of the fall

River of Sweet Water

Nothing is lost
in translation
The clarity between
us is distinct
Wants and needs
are defined.
A wall was never
built from the beginning
Perhaps that's why
there is a river
between us
The love we have
for each other
drips sweet water
This is how we created
the river of sweet water

Radiant Insomnia

I am threaded up
in radiant insomnia
replaying your
precious voice

I am entwined
in the details of
your lush fabric

I am intoxicated
in the essence of
your twilight soul

I am thunderstruck
in the golden trees
under your shining stars

I am trying to close
my eyes and feel
your magical skin

Italicized Kindness

Inexplicably enhanced
and distinguished
Incredibly distinctive
and profound
Kindness is italicized
A rare breed
One of a kind
Embracing humanity
Displaying compassion
Simple greetings
A lost instinctive art
Masses becoming selfish
"One nation under God"
is just a line in an oath
Kindness should be italicized

Falling into Twilight

Love her precious sky
Love her southern wind
Love her gentle soul
Love her divine tenderness
Fall into her light

Love her brilliant heart
Love her rare body
Love her stunning mind
Love her candlelit intuition
Fall into her wildflower

Love her innocent giggle
Love her inner child
Love her broken moon
Love her bashful sun
Fall into twilight

Breathtaking Religion

I demand to taste
your language of sensuality
I hunger for your
education on my lips
I'm pining for your
words of acknowledgement
I have a sweet tooth
for your delicious nectar
I have a soft spot
for your overflowing words
I embrace your
magic dancing off your tongue
I cherish the essence
of your breathtaking religion

Forever in the Afterglow

I want to suffocate in your bliss
I want to plunge into your beloved river
I want to soak up your sincerity
Open and let me find you

I fell for your afterglow
I want to be overwhelmed by your eyes
I want to sink in your palm
I want to be strangled by your affection
Open and let me see you

I fell for your silver tongue
I want to be enthralled by your charm
I want to consume your high flames
I want to sleep between your light and dark
Open and let me feel you

I fell for your enchanting universe
I want to soak up your character
I want to touch your insecurities
I want to kiss your lips of heaven
Open and let me listen to you

I fell for your wisdom dripping from you

Blanket of Tenderness

Snuggling and up close
Conversations thicken like fog
Hand in hand
Covered up in affection
Comfortably sizzling
Love is like a blanket of tenderness
Refusing to remove
Wrapped up in the roses of eternity
Senses heightened and gripped
Endless desires and hopes
Kissing and caressing faith
Clasping on to your whispers
Brushing up against your smile
Clutching every memory created
Never letting go of unconditional love

Beauty of Reflection

Love your wounds
Love your beloved shine
Love your stunning beauty
Love your angelic smile
Love your tender spirit
Love your lost soul
Love your endearing glow
Love your deep scars
Love your vibrant class
Love your intelligence
Love your shape
Love your magnificent truth
Love your elegance
Love your fallen tears
Love your curiosity
Love your complexity
Love your drive
Love your amazing identity

Singapore Dove

The Singapore dove dashes
Sparkles of a warmth soar
Throats of innocence tingle
In awe of the simplicity
Raptured up in its tenderness
Captured by its soft touch
Rivers and creeks entwine
Thirsty for your embrace
Breathing in your kindness
Fantasies slowly ripple
Shadows of your body glow
Immeasurable beauty stares
Inhale your crystal elegance
the cerulean sky
Seeking the Singapore Dove

Piece of Peace

I coddle your insecurities
I enshrine your mystique
I honor your brittle bones
I worship your flexibility
I cultivate your music
I venerate your strength
I idolize your piece of peace
I praise your intuition
I savor your wildfire
I treasure your skeletons
I indulge in your core
I love your masked shadows
I clutch to your wisdom
I harbor your piece of peace

Weeping Daydreams

In your arms
I felt the shine of the sun
In your arms
I felt the overjoyed love
In your arms
I felt the emptiness fade
In your arms
I felt the perfect embrace
In your arms
I felt the daydreams weep love
In your arms
I felt our worlds be complete
In your arms
I felt us melt as one
In your arms
I felt your precious tears
In your arms
I felt our life begin

Vows to an Angel

I stood between the dusk
and the shimmering light
I stared at the crescent of
the bellowing moons

As I sat there in a moment
of reflection
I could feel the teardrops of
an angel falls on my shoulder

She was more radiant
than a painting
She was more elegant
than a statue of gold

I fell in love with her
crying shadows
I fell in love with her
loneliness and cravings

As my hand touched
her cheekbone
I was overcome by joy
Fulfilled every threshold
of my beating and still heart

On bended knee
I wept in the river of love
Overflowing and cleansed
I reached for my quill
and the words poured out
like the rain from the bleeding sky

My undying love for a fallen angel
was cemented in my vows
Embraced in forever
Cherishing her like a poem

Placing the diamond on her
porcelain finger
Gentle like a china doll
Eternal flames surround our unity
Endlessly in love with a perfect soul

Satin Moonlight

Exhausted from the breathtaking gust
Replaying all the motions
of the perfect night
Mesmerized by her soothing moans
Our entangled bodies merged
The unspoken dance curved into a
ballad I can't shut off inside myself
The satin moonlight was held in
our fingertips
Words never uttered under the covers
Only blissful flames and never ending
appetites
Louis Armstrong playing in my
right ear
Dinah Washington playing in my
left ear
Caressing the tender sunrise as I gaze
at her magnificence
Love was etched from the melody
Not the unwritten lyrics

In My Dreams

Heart stopping and astonishing
A wondrous ray of shine
Spine tingling and thrilling
An extraordinary spirit
Loving her twinkle
Electrifying and rip-roaring
A stimulating dove in the clouds
Provocative and sensational
An impressive personality
First class and remarkable
Loving her morning rain
A lightning center
Spectacular and unbelievable
A miracle for my eyes
Marvelous and staggering
A beautiful human being
She's out there somewhere
Or just in my dreams

Breathtaking Lullaby

She has guided his tears into the desert to dry
She has laid beside him to calm the fears
She sang a heartfelt lullaby to soothe his spirit
She had the voice of an angel
He couldn't thank her enough
A revelation is pronounced.
He kisses her on the forehead
She breathes in the silence of love and admiration
A new beginning was born
The comfort that they shared was priceless
He opened more than he wanted
She listened and it was needed
The tenderness dripped from her fingertips
He stared into her soft magnetic eyes
It started with a breathtaking lullaby

Treasuring Your Magic

I want to kiss your tears
I want to hold your sorrows in my palms
I want to clench onto you like a pearl
I want to feel the edges of your stars
I want to gaze into your treasured eyes
I want to feel your darkest night
I want to sip from your cup of determination
I want to feel your magic on my fingertips
I want to embrace your wildfire and shine
I want to be on your precious canvas
I want to remember your liquid touch
I want to feel the bricks of your crumbled walls
I want to drink from your humble knowledge

Sweet Adoration

I adore you like
the sky adores the birds
I adore you like
the sand adores the ocean
I adore you like
the cheeks adore the wind
I adore you like
the cement adores the rain
I adore you like
the flowers adore the sun
I adore you like
the moon adores the night
I adore you like
the leaves adore the trees
I adore you like
the pillows adore the bed
I adore you like
I never have before

Crooked Thunderbolts

Under a rainbow of shades of blue
I saw a glimpse of your golden smile
Staring at your freckles
I gaze into the storms of your eyes
Embracing crooked thunderbolts
I fell into your theatrical mist
Touching your sapphire core
I stumbled into a haze of echoing beauty
Repeating your name in my sleep
I adore your quiet skeletons
Admiring your drops of anguish
I hold you delicately in my arms
Falling madly in love with your spirit

Arm's Length

I'm irrelevant
I'm not on anyone's mind
I'm not in your thoughts
I must think grand to exist
I swim alone in my own ocean
I walk through the silent creek
I can see tar in my soul
I stand under a dying wing
I'm the dark cloud in the storm
I keep everyone at arm's length
To avoid to feel

Once in a Lifetime

I'm terrified
to inhale your naked skies
I'm terrified
to kiss your illuminating scars
I'm terrified
to wipe away your violent tears
I'm terrified
to capture your torn heart
I'm terrified
to feel your dirty rain
I'm terrified
to hold on to your numb hand
I'm terrified
to feel a love that I didn't know existed
I'm terrified
to hear the symphony in your sea
I'm terrified
to walk alone on this broken road
I'm terrified
to stand at the turns in this landscape

Deep Love

Deep love doesn't surrender
Deep love forgives
Deep love is a tornado of passion
Deep love forever glows
Deep love is sweet candy
Deep love is wide open
Deep love is a silent wind
Deep love is a burning rush
Deep love is always ignited
Deep love has a gold frame
Deep love has twinkling magic
Deep love never fades
Deep love doesn't have glitter
Deep love doesn't leave you empty

Valiant Embrace

Sprinkle me a sunset
Dazzle me with a light mist
Entice me with your kindness
Lure me with your sensuality
Pull me in with your warmth
Cover me with conversation
Warm me by the candlelight
Love me with your mind
Dress me in your perfume
Cleanse me with your purity
Find me your dreamscape
Feel our shining valiant embrace

Perfect Match

Quite exceptional
Alluring to the center
Leathered and worn
But a hand in glove
A gravitational pull
Never ending thoughts
Captivating wonder
But a hand in glove
Intensified curiosity
An endless thirst
An honest spirit
But a hand in glove
Kind and generous
Absolutely gorgeous
A magical desire
But a hand in glove

Awestruck

Glazed by your
delightful fragrance
Loves struck by your
tender caress
Daydreaming of your
traditional heart
Admiring your
glowing purity
Cherishing the
taste of your tears
Appreciating your
strong backbone

Empathy Soars

Empathy soars
As I listen to your song
No drug can
take away your endless pain
Tears flowing hard
from my eyes
Not yours
You lost an extension
No one can be
his replacement
If you had a man
like that
It shows you are
worthy of a real man
Don't compare
No one will ever be him
For a moment
I put myself in your shoes
I can feel the cement
and the empathy soars

The Pillow's Scent

I can't sleep
without the scent of your pillow
Toss and turn
I can't sleep
without you beside me
Toss and turn
I can't sleep
without your warm embrace
Toss and turn
I can't sleep
without a kiss good night
Toss and turn
I can't sleep
without saying I love you
Toss and turn

Basket of Gold

Hand in hand
Walking through the basket of gold
Surrounded by nature's scent
Barefoot and carefree
Like the precious love in our hearts
Hand in hand
Gripping tight refusing to let go
Appreciating the sound of her voice
Marveled by her addicting laughter
Whispering "PS I love you"
In her ear and kissing her neck
Under the hundred-year oak tree
Hand in hand
Realizing this hand is the only hand
I want to feel for a lifetime

Tight Grip

Hold my grey agony
In your arms
Hold my silent wounds
In your arms
Please don't let go
Hold my crying tenderness
In your arms
Hold my wild yearnings
In your arms
Please don't let go
Hold my precious love
In your arms
Hold my shadows of darkness
In your arms
Please don't let go
Hold my overpowering weakness
In your arms
Hold my wide-open skies
In your arms
Please don't let go

Crescendo Sky

Melodies drifting
through a sound breeze
Violins serenading
a chilling winters morning
Ghosts parading
surrounding a glorious symphony
Peasants kneeling
to an omnipotent voice
Praising and crying
thankful and grateful
Lilacs dancing
Waterfalls praying
angels weeping
Under Gods crescendo sky

Crumpled up Letter

Crumpled up letters
Sobbing in hysterics
In a dismal empty room
A 60-watt lightbulb
brightens up the corner
leaving my sorrows
to drown and crawl
in the mourning black
Detesting the fury
in the restless ink
Quickly the door opens
Ignoring your hollow
and oversized sermon
Shaking my tired head
to your diluted church
Justifying her passing
Reminding me
"Everything will be okay"
Biting my angry tongue
pulling out the letter
to my almighty God
"Why God Why"
Undiscovered answers
hang in the picture
of my dear beautiful mother

Paper God

Constricted thoughts
Sterile and hazy emptiness
Extracting her vertebrae
Wallowing in a glossy prison
On troubled and dented knees
Praying to a paper God
Dwelling in the unanswered
Commanding the stage
Not comprehending lack
of guided presence
Outraged and shouting
a pile of obscenities
Not separating the distinction
between faith and belief

The Blush Vertebrae

Icicles of vulnerability
dangle over my crucified nerves
Leisurely indulging
a mass consumption of integrity
Thickening the backbone
Watching frustrations corrode
Tortuously eyeballing the poison
seep in my blush vertebrae
Struggling between the roar of
disarray and the calm light
Hacking up chunks of sincerity
Clearing my throat to voice
the sound of everlasting waves
from my vibrant spine
Drops of sorrow fall to my feet
Faith never misled my center

Presence

I crossed
the paths I could not see
I glided
on the horizon I could feel
I carved
out my castles in the carnival
I escaped
the memories I couldn't feel
I paraded
the streets of prayers
I walked
alone searching for a hand
I thanked
you for being invisible
I wanted
you to fulfill my addiction
I needed
to see the bottom to find the truth
I woke
up from the touch of your hand
I smiled
because God was there the entire time

Embrace

Embrace the rain
Embrace the tears
Embrace every second
Embrace the laughter
Embrace the scent of the flowers
Embrace every minute
Embrace the pain
Embrace the joys of love
Embrace the hours
Embrace the rollercoaster
Embrace the turns
Embrace the moments
Embrace your family and friends
Embrace the love making
Embrace making love
Embrace the time of your life

September Crawls

September crawls from the closet of rusted chains
The amber flag waves above the barn and doesn't forget
Leaves of melancholy fall silently to the dusty spiritless ground
The church around the corner of my fortress is empty
I am on my knees bound to eternity praying to a God painted on a window
September crawls from the wall of poison fears
The pen on the desk bleeds ink and never remembers my rhyme patterns
Winds of sadness only blow east to rattle my distant mind
The scripture in the Bible is wrapped around my cold point of view
I am on my knees caged to religion praying to a God that I don't understand
I am engaged to spirituality not religion

www.ingramcontent.com/pod-product-compliance
Lightning Source LLC
Chambersburg PA
CBHW031156270326
41931CB00006B/297
* 9 7 8 1 7 3 4 7 4 9 9 0 8 *